# The Ladder of Evil Revealed

Jane Snyder

Founder/CEO Melchizedek's Treasure Ltd

Founder/Trustee Active Blessing Uganda NGO

Founder Active Blessing International Coalition

ISBN-13: 978-1499545500
ISBN-10: 1499545509

# DEDICATION

Dedicated to a dear friend and supporter, Dr. Richard "Woodie" Waters with whom I first shared this book.

His comment was, " This is just a teaching. Where's the story? Out of all of those Africa stories you publish in your newsletters, isn't there one for this book?"

So here is one for you Woodie!

# CONTENTS

# ACKNOWLEDGMENTS

I love writing "the revealed wisdom of God" because of its' similarity to music and the arts. It has substance, revelation, form, beauty, and loveliness, to name just a few of its' attributes. But most important of all, it contains the power of God within it, waiting for the agreement of a human heart. With human agreement to its' truth, the power of God is released into the realm of the spiritual and natural world and "evil" is dealt another blow. This acknowledgment is to the Holy Spirit for its unseen and potentially powerful work, waiting upon your activation.

I wish to thank my wonderful editor Terry DeSeta, who was both professional and a great pleasure to work with. I treasure our times together spent on those extended phone calls after her long day at work. I appreciate your sacrifice Terry. Thank-You...

A mother's heartfelt appreciation goes to Jesse Snyder, who gave me a Mothers Day gift of putting this book on its' template. And to Bob Snyder for showing me how to write a poem!

Many of you will appreciate John Munns and the Therapon ministry, for his graphics and detailed exploration of the "Redeemed" and "Unredeemed" human heart, within the Epilogue.

# PREFACE

EVIL .... ITS WORK.... AND HOW TO STOP IT

This short book has been generated from one word: BLAME. That word was given to me one morning as I was getting out of bed. It was a normal day, with nothing exceptional on the horizon. I had been at war "on the ground" for a very long time, against great evil, in my work with street kids in Uganda, and the attacks we were ceaselessly enduring had strangely begun to feel normal. Evil exposed hates the light, and we had exposed much evil.

Our little organization in Uganda was suffering much loss in every way, starting with physical loss of property, of beloved personnel, of our reputation, and a few of our supporters. We had enemies who hated us, and were active in their destruction. They had laid siege and were triumphing over us. The money necessary to keep our thirty street pastors from suffering had gone dry. They were sick, worn, attacked, needy, and unable to do their ministry, and it was breaking my heart. I would tell them, "Hold on. Help will come. Don't give up". I was speaking what I knew to be true, but at the same time, everything in me wanted just to blame something. I found myself searching for the right target to point the finger at, and there were too many to count! It is so much easier to cope if there is someone or something to accuse. It is easy to blame the 'bad guys', because they deserve it, and there were plenty of 'bad guys' around!

I went to my computer and placed the word BLAME on the page, and suddenly saw a picture of the evil kingdom as a series of rungs on a ladder, with blame as a crucial beginning. Understanding was instantly given to me as I saw the operation of these steps of evil in the world. I saw their activity in major events such as mass destruction, as well as in the quiet sin in an individual's heart. This sentence was then spoken to me: "Blame is the step where evil can be stopped." Immediately I thought, "I have been given a great treasure of knowledge for the Body of Christ." And I knew that this treasure is meant not only for my personal life and ministry, but also for the furtherance of Jesus' ministry in our world as the Prince of Peace.

In the following pages I will try to describe this "Ladder of Evil", along with examples from my own life and ministry. I will also give some strategies for victory over the enemy of our souls. My hope and prayer is that it will bring greater power to the Body of Christ for defanging the evil we have allowed to flourish through our willingness to blame, and that this 'ladder' revelation can be used for awareness, for freedom, and for help in promoting the REAL Prince of Peace.

> Mat 5:9 Blessed are the peacemakers for they shall be called the sons of God.

# INTRODUCTION

## THE EVIL KINGDOM'S LADDER:

5. Death.......The ultimate goal of every ladder step.

4. Destruction........................Easiest path to death

3. Anger.................The force necessary to produce violence and destruction.

2. Blame....................................The focus for anger

1. Evil Manifesting..............Evil displayed in the world

We live in a fallen world full of self-propagating, manifesting evil. The ladder shows the steps that evil takes to bring its result of great suffering into our world. If not stopped, evil ends through death, in hell itself—the ultimate goal. But there is a weak link in this evil progression - it needs our cooperation, or agreement, to continue its course. Evil can be stopped by how we respond to it--at ladder step number two--Blame!

The picture given me was of evil splashing out from each rung of the ladder into the world. I will try to describe the splashing I saw, though it is hard to illustrate spiritual impressions.

## SPLASHING

### From step one: Manifesting Evil

I first saw horrible displays of evil, such as violent crimes, murders, wars, and rebel groups with no real agendas except destruction. Individual people were being used in ways they weren't even aware of, until the outcomes revealed the agenda.

### From step two: Blame

I then saw blame for these outcomes

cast about in every conversation, and in the daily news.

**From step three: Anger**

Next I saw the whole world, because of blame, angry with each other. Heads of state could not even function because of the amount of virulent anger generated, and revenge threats were the order of the day.

**From step four: Destruction**

After this I saw numerous countries degenerating into shambles--without government, law, or order.

**From step five: Death**

Finally, I saw the result of the unbelieving world's fateful choice -hell. It is the final, irrevocable separation from God, from life, and from all goodness. This, of course, is satan's wicked plan.

All of this destruction will pave the way for the anti-Christ to come and rescue the world from its own horror, and this false savior will be the world's answer. The real path of life must be preached to the whole world, for only then will the end come with God's grand and good plan. Those who believe in Christ will not fall prey to the deception that will totally ensnare the world. That great deception is that the anti-christ himself is coming as the savior, to "save the world" from the terrible destruction splashing down from the ladder of evil!

We who are in the body of Christ must offer them Jesus' way out of the evil agenda, on the rung of "Blame", ladder step two. This revelation is the very point of the book. As we continue, I will include and expand upon the ladder in each chapter, with special emphasis placed upon step two, hoping by this to give it more power in your memory. But I will begin each chapter with a true story from Africa that beautifully illustrates the ladder of evil, and the victory that can be won by the path of escape that has been made through Jesus Christ.

> John 10:10 Jesus said: The thief comes only to **steal** and **kill** and **destroy**; I came that they may have life, and have it abundantly.

# 1. EVIL MANIFESTING

**The Ladder:**

5. Death

4. Destruction

3. Anger

2. Blame

1. **Evil Manifesting**

## Our Story Begins:

This is the true story of one of my Ugandan street pastors I'll call Todd. His job is to evangelize street kids, to keep watch over them and to represent their interests when they are exploited. His report to me begins here, and will continue throughout each chapter.

> "Mom, since I got sick, I had taken a lot of time without checking on my kids on streets, because I was seriously sick and almost dead. But just by the grace of the Lord who brought you to me, giving me life again through spending a lot of money on my medical treatment, I am now healed and back on streets. May God bless you. I started working this week fully with strength, because I have been very weak since I got sick. But God has given me authority and wisdom over many things, and power to punish the devil.
>
> Yesterday morning I was called to save a young street kid boy who had spent 15 hours on tree, tied on, by a bad man who is known by the whole village as the best witch doctor, and he had practiced witchcraft for all of his life. He had killed a

lot of people for no reasons, and no one could attack him or tell him if he is doing anything wrong. He thought he was smarter than everyone in this village and had announced to kill the whole village and remain alone in that village. No one could attack him and even police were fearing this man. He is still killing people and he has been a very great giant Satan.

## LADDER STEP 1: EVIL MANIFESTING

Evil manifests in two ways:

1. Personal

   Coming into us from the outside, making us the victim of its inherent pain.

   Coming from inside us, expressed outwardly toward others, making them the victim of our blame and anger.

2. Corporate

   Evil gains power through agreement with its agenda. It can then erupt into wars, catastrophes and spreadable diseases, both from natural and spiritual sources.

The first ladder step, caused by the evil originating in human hearts, is used by the devil as he seeks to exploit any kind of pain for the growth of blame. In it is contained the 'food' to feed the ladder and make it self-perpetuating. Evil's favorite tool is deception.

## THE FIRST FAMILY AND THE LADDER OF EVIL

In the book of Genesis, the story of the first family is a poignant history lesson of the formation of the evil ladder in the earth.

### STEP 1..... EVIL MANIFESTING IN THE WORLD

Gen.3:1 Now the serpent was more crafty than any beast of the field which the LORD God had made. And he said to the woman, "Indeed, has God said, 'You shall not eat from any tree of the garden?'"

### STEP 2 .... BLAME

Gen. 3:12 The man said, "The woman whom You gave to be with me, she gave me from the tree, and I ate." 13 Then the LORD God said to the woman, "What is this you have done?" And the woman said, "The serpent deceived me, and I ate."

## STEP 3 .... ANGER

Gen.4:5 but for Cain and for his offering He had
no regard. So Cain became very angry and his
countenance fell. 6 Then the LORD said to
Cain, “Why are you angry? And why has your
countenance fallen? 7 If you do well, will not
your countenance be lifted up? And if you do
not do well, sin is crouching at the door; and
its desire is for you, but you must master it.”

## STEP 4 .... DESTRUCTION

Gen.4:8a And it came about when they were in the field, that Cain rose up against Abel his brother...

## STEP 5 .... DEATH

Gen. 4:8b ....and killed him.

## THE ESCAPE ....

Gen. 5:28 Adam had relations with his wife
again; and she gave birth to a son, and named
him Seth, for, she said, “God has appointed me
another offspring in place of Abel, for Cain
killed him.” 26 To Seth, to him also a son was
born; and he called his name Enosh. Then men
began to call upon the name of the LORD.

When Jesus walked upon the earth, He showed His Lordship over personal and corporate evil by:

- Healing and delivering people

  Example: Mt.4:24 The news about Him (Jesus) spread throughout all Syria; and they brought to Him all who were ill, those suffering with various diseases and pains, demoniacs, epileptics, paralytics; and He healed them.

- Stilling the storm Mt.8:23-25
- Walking on water Mt.14:26
- Producing needed money from the inside of a fish Mt. 17:27
- Multiplying one person's lunch to feed 4000 people Mk 6:41
- Appearing supernaturally Acts1:3

He was Lord over natural physical laws, but he was not yet Lord over the Evil Ladder. Victory would come to a roaring conclusion after the crucifixion, when He took the keys of death and hades from the devil in His new resurrected body. We will explore this in detail in chapter six, The Path of Escape.

# 2. BLAME

**The Ladder:**

5. Death

4. Destruction

3. Anger

2. **Blame**

1. Evil Manifesting

## Todd's Story Continues:

"I was called yesterday to come see this tied boy, and when I reached at the boy he was very badly beaten and he had blood everywhere and was still on the tree fainted. I cried tears when I set my eyes on this boy of 8 yrs. and I just saw how much this man had behaved like an animal. I thought of how I was going to face him and tell him what he was doing was wrong, yet the boy was BLAMED to be stealing in this man's garden and not once.

I went back home to take a bath from my work on streets as street pastor, but instead I began to think many things about how to save the boy because he was too young to deserve such a punishment even if he had stolen. I worshipped in 2 songs and I had a prayer asking God to lead on the way, as I go and save this boy, because I just knew he was still alive. I went to see this man and we have a talk at least.

Upon reaching his home he told me before I step in his yard, that I will not be talking and it will be against my life, so I better be careful if I am to tamper with him by trespassing at his home. I strongly told him, “You man, God has led me from where I sleep to come and see you because God still wants to give you a second chance and he loves you as his son.“

And when I said that, he asked me, “Who are you? Where do you come from? Which type of gods do you worship?”

I told him, “I worship the Most High God and He is the Creator of heaven and earth.

Man asked, “And what do you want at my place, such a person who does not fear me in this village?”

I told him, ”I have come for the life of the young boy who is dying on the tree.”

The man told me, “The boy is already dead and I want to use his body and I will not give it to anyone. This boy has been stealing me.”

I told him, “God is giving the boy the second chance of having life again.”

The man told me, "With the magic I have done, he has no second chance, and if you think your God can make a miracle and he wakes up and goes with you, then try your best."

I told him, "Fine." And I started worshipping again as I was going towards the boy. I untied him, and put him down, and started praying for him. And Lord my God was with me, and the boy waked up from the coma. The whole village was watching what was going on and even the man was also seeing what was going on.

I got the boy up after praying for him and I told this man, "My God needs you and you should get saved from your evil, and you will be the best man of my God I worship." He stood and looked at me as i was going with the boy and the whole village thanked me for what i had done.

Today the man came to me and got saved from his evil.

Mom, I am sorry to get lost from you for so long but I want to let you know that I have been busy working everyday since God last saved that young boy

from death. Everyone in this village takes me like God's messenger or savior sent from heaven, and I have been praying for many people and many have accepted Jesus as their Lord and Savior. I have noted their names down and they are in the number of 200 going above. The boy, the one you helped with some medical treatment after I got him down from the tree and out of the village, said thank you so much and he is wishing to see you.
Your son, T"

## LADDER STEP 2: BLAME

The manifestation of evil leads to blame, since the natural reaction of the human heart is to believe that something or someone has to be held accountable for any kind of pain. This is the Evil Kingdom's starting platform; the point at which evil becomes internalized into the individual or corporate soul, and it is here the upward ladder climb begins.

**Blame is the place where we can stop our participation in the evil agenda.** We must refuse to blame.

Let us explore: **The Three Directions of Blame**

1. Blame Others ….. such as: bad guys, institutions, governments, rebel armies, race, gender, religions, devil, etc.

2. Blame God ….. such as: You could have stopped this; A good God would not allow this evil. I trusted You. You don't care. I hate You. You caused this hurricane that destroyed everything.

3. Blame Self ….. such as: I caused this; I am no good; If it wasn't for me this would not have happened; I could have done more; I didn't do enough; I should have stopped this; Why didn't I see it? Why didn't I help him?

**Blame Contains:**

Choices, Excuses, Agreements, Judgments, and Accusations.

Choices: We choose who or what to condemn based upon our prejudices. We prefer lies and deceptions, that allows self to be manipulated into Blame. A great example is how Eve chose to believe the deception and lie from the serpent in the Garden of Eden; "You will not surely die." Genesis 3:4 When God had already made it plain that the consequence would be death.

Excuses: We make excuses for our sin, such as: And the woman said, "The serpent deceived me, and I ate." Genesis3:13

Agreements: We believe in, and take action, that bring Blame to the next ladder step, Anger. When we choose Blame, we are agreeing with satan's perspective on the situation.

Judgments: Our judgments may or may not be righteous by God's standards.

Accusations: Accusing is the outward result of inward blame. One of the names of satan is "accuser".

> Revelation 12:10 I heard a loud voice in heaven, saying, "Now the salvation, and the power, and the kingdom of our God and the authority of His Christ have come, for the **accuser** of our brethren has been thrown down, **he who accuses them** before our God day and night.

## What To Do Instead of Blame

The ultimate stop to evil is to **forgive** the person/ tribe/ institution/ nation/ etc. that is perpetuating the evil.

I think that we can acknowledge that forgiveness is something too hard to manage without Jesus Christ in our hearts. To come to the place where we can acknowledge that we even SHOULD forgive can take much thought and soul searching. It is so much easier and natural to find a reason to blame instead.

Yet... God Says:

> Acts 26:18 "...to open their eyes, in order to turn them from darkness to light, and from the power of Satan to God, that they may receive **forgiveness** of sins and an inheritance among those who are sanctified by faith in Me."
>
> Daniel 9:9 "To the Lord our God belong mercy and **forgiveness**, though we have rebelled against Him."
>
> Mark 11:25 "And whenever you stand praying, if you have anything against anyone, **forgive** him, that your Father in heaven may also **forgive** you your trespasses.
>
> Psalm 130:4 But there is **forgiveness** with You, (God) that You may be feared.

# 3. ANGER

5. Death

4.Destruction

**3.Anger**

2.Blame (You can get off the ladder right here by forgiveness)

1. Evil manifesting

**Our Story Continues:**

I, Jane, arrived in Africa to check on our street pastors only to learn that this brave soul Todd was nowhere close to his own city and job, but was instead living on the streets as a street kid, in a city he had never been to before, on the other side of the country. I was shocked and angry, and when I finally caught up with him, I demanded, "What are you doing here?" He would not answer me. I found someone who knew Todd, and asked him what was going on that no one was telling me. I was told to wait, and he would come to see me and explain everything.

After a few days Todd came to my hotel room and quietly told me his story, a most terrible story of hatred and revenge. He had been having great success in the area, bringing hundreds of people to faith in Jesus Christ. But even more significantly, Todd had also brought to freedom the area's most powerful witch doctor, a man with a deep family allegiance to and control by these evil spirits, stretching back many generations. Liberating the witch-doctor inevitably unleashed the spirits' wrath and quick revenge. As they saw it, these hundreds of souls, and worse, this mighty witch-doctor, had been stolen by Todd and removed from their kingdom, losing them an invaluable tool in their unholy plans. Todd had come from a family famous for its long-standing supremacy in dominating the people. In retaliation these spirits incited child-traffickers to capture two more street kids. Todd went to save them, but this time he failed.

Todd's story produced its desired effect in me by making me hate those traffickers. The anger was boiling inside me, and here I was in the process of writing this nice book! And though I could plainly see it, I didn't even care about my obvious hypocrisy, I was so angry at the "bad guys"!

## LADDER STEP 3: ANGER

The resolution of anger is much more difficult than stopping your responses at step 2, Blame. Anger has power and the ability to morph into different avenues of destruction. This is why blame is the best place to get off of the Ladder of Evil.

Anger is an emotion characterized by antagonism toward someone or something you feel has deliberately done you wrong. It contains the raw power to escalate step 2 Blame to step 4 Destruction. Anger loves to use threats to accomplish its agendas, and a threat's mental bondage is stronger than chains. I have chosen some Webster Dictionary definitions to help us gain insight into different forms of anger such as hatred, bitterness, rage and wrath, as all of these are escalating steps from anger to destruction.

**Hatred** is built-up anger.

prejudiced hostility or animosity <old racial prejudices and national hatreds>

**Bitterness** is internalized anger.

a : accompanied by severe pain or suffering <a bitter death>

c : exhibiting intense animosity <bitter enemies>

d (1) : harshly reproachful <bitter complaints> (2) : marked by cynicism and rancor <bitter contempt>

e: expressive of severe pain, grief, or regret <bitter tears>

**Rage** is expressed anger taking its victim directly to violence and destruction.

a : violent and uncontrolled anger

b : a fit of violent wrath

c archaic : insanity

**Wrath** - expressed revenge

a : strong vengeful anger or indignation

b : retributory punishment for an offense or a crime : divine chastisement

## THE THREE TYPES OF ANGER

Anger is of course experienced both in a collective sense and within all people individually. It is also found in God, and His anger is just. Following are explanations of collective, individual, and God's anger:

### Collective Anger

Collective anger has huge destructive potential for the ladder of evil, and it can be passed down from generation to generation in such attitudes as tribal prejudice and mistrust, which often produce rebel groups and hostile take-overs. Group dynamics built around a cause are another form of collective anger, and the following passage is a report from my new book: Street Kids Speak, which shows an incident of this kind of collective anger and the way it was dealt with. I am not giving any judgment on how it was managed; I am just using it as an example of collective anger.

**Pastor's Report**

"The slums of Soroti Town, Uganda, in early March was such an ungodly time because there were lots of crimes which included theft, especially breaking into shops and restaurants and late night rape around night clubs.

So the police were asked by the community to explain why there are rampant theft and rape cases. The only reason they gave was that the street kids were the source of all the crimes because they had highly increased in number in these particular slums. So they decided to make operations in an attempt to capture street kids.... This is when the street kids waged war against the police and any other stranger that went near them.

The street kids became so hostile to an extent that they were moving with stones and on seeing the police, they would throw stones at them. At night they would retreat to their gangs to discuss the calamity that had befallen them and how best they could defeat their enemy [police]. I took trouble to talk to four of the gang leaders on the matter but they all denied the accusation saying they didn't steal. But surely they were proved innocent when the real criminals were arrested and the he war came to an end."

## Personal Anger

Anger within an individual can also cause great harm, and is something we deal with throughout our lives. As the story at the beginning of this chapter shows, *"Todd's story produced its desired effect in me by making me hate those traffickers."* My anger was something I had to confront and deal with, if I was to stay off the ladder of evil.

## God's Anger---Justice

In this chapter study we are looking at anger as part of an evil agenda. But we must also recognize that righteous anger--God's kind of anger-- can be a good thing. It can give a way to express negative feelings about wrongs suffered. It can also be a motivation to find solutions to problems, or even to seek justice. Without its power, nothing of righteousness would be accomplished!

How does God deal with His anger? We see a good example of righteous anger in the bible story of Jesus cleansing the temple. Jesus' anger had reached the stage of wrath (divine chastisement) at the money-changers conducting their business in the outer court of the temple, and He had no hesitation in expressing it!

> Luke 19:45 Taking a whip He drove them out saying, “My Father’s House is to be a house of prayer for all nations!”

> Numbers 14:18 ‘The Lord is slow to **anger** and abundant in loving-kindness, forgiving iniquity and transgression; but He will by no means clear the guilty, visiting the iniquity of the fathers on the children to the third and the fourth generations.’

## HELP IN DEALING WITH ANGER

We all struggle with processing anger, so I

want to offer some individual help in the study of this topic. The Bible makes it clear that it is not something to ignore. For example:

> Ecclesiastes 11:10 So, remove grief and **anger** from your heart and put away pain from your body, because childhood and the prime of life are fleeting.

The American Psychological Association says there are three main approaches that people can take to curb their anger. These approaches are expressing, suppressing, and calming.

**Expressing:**

Anger is a natural, adaptive response to threats; it inspires powerful, often aggressive, feelings and behaviors, which allow us to fight and to defend ourselves when we are attacked. A certain amount of anger, therefore, is necessary for our survival.

On the other hand, we can't physically lash out at every person or object that irritates or annoys us; laws, social norms, and common sense place limits on how far our anger can take us. People use a variety of both conscious and unconscious processes to deal with their angry feelings.

Expressing your angry feelings in an assertive—but not aggressive—manner is the healthiest way to express anger. To do this, you have to learn how to make clear what your needs are, and how to get them met, without hurting others. Being assertive doesn't mean being pushy or demanding; it means being respectful of yourself and others. 1.

> Colossians 3:8 But now you also, put them all aside: **anger**, wrath, malice, slander, and abusive speech from your mouth.

> Micah 7:18 Who is a God like You, who pardons iniquity and passes over the rebellious act of the remnant of His possession? He does not retain His **anger** forever, because He delights in unchanging love.

**Suppressing:**

Anger can be suppressed, and then converted or redirected. This happens when you hold in your anger, stop thinking about it, and focus on something positive. The aim is to inhibit or suppress your anger and convert it into more constructive behavior. The danger in this type of response is that if it isn't allowed outward expression, your anger can turn inward—on yourself. Anger turned inward may cause hypertension, high blood pressure, or depression.

Unexpressed anger can create other problems. It can lead to pathological expressions of anger, such as passive-aggressive behavior (getting back at people indirectly, without telling them why, rather than confronting them head-on) or a personality that seems perpetually cynical and hostile. People who are constantly putting others down, criticizing everything, and making cynical comments haven't learned how to constructively express their anger. Not surprisingly, they aren't likely to have many successful relationships. 2

> Proverbs 15:1 A gentle answer turns away wrath, but a harsh word stirs up **anger**.
>
> Proverbs 16:32 He who is slow to **anger** is better than the mighty, and he who rules his spirit, than he who captures a city.

**Calming:**

Finally, you can calm down inside. This means not just controlling your outward behavior, but also controlling your internal responses, taking steps to lower your heart rate, calm yourself down, and let the feelings subside.

As Dr. Spielberger notes, "when none of these three techniques work, that's when someone—or something—is going to get hurt.

It's best to find out what triggers your anger. Angry people tend to curse, swear, or speak in highly colorful terms that reflect their inner thoughts. Try redirecting with a simple prayer for calming and more logical thinking. 3

## GOD'S WISDOM CONCERNING ANGER

Psalm 37:8 Cease from **anger** and forsake wrath; Do not fret; it leads only to evildoing.

Proverbs 22:24 Do not associate with a man given to **anger**; or go with a hot-tempered man.

Ephesians 4:26 Be angry, and yet do not sin; do not let the sun go down on your **anger.**

Galatians 5:19-21 Now the deeds of the flesh are evident, which are: immorality, impurity, sensuality, idolatry, sorcery, enmities, strife, jealousy, **outbursts of anger**, disputes, dissensions, factions, envying, drunkenness, carousing, and things like these, of which I forewarn you, just as I have forewarned you, that those who practice such things will not inherit the kingdom of God.

Matthew 5:22 But I say to you that everyone who is **angry** with his brother shall be guilty before the court; and whoever says to his brother, 'You good-for-nothing,' shall be guilty before the supreme court; and whoever says, 'You fool,' shall be guilty enough to go into the fiery hell.

Job 36:13 "But the godless in heart lay up **anger**; they do not cry for help when He binds them.

Ephesians 4:31 Let all bitterness and wrath and **anger** and clamor and slander be put away from you, along with all malice.

Proverbs 29:8 Scorners set a city aflame, but wise men turn away **anger**.

[1]

[1] 1.Fact Sheet (January 2005 © 2014 American
2. Ibid

3. Ibid

# 4. DESTRUCTION

5. Death

**4. Destruction**

3. Anger

2. Blame (You can get off the ladder right here by forgiveness)

1. Evil manifesting

## Our Story Continues:

The child-traffickers took Todd's two street kids, and slaughtered them in front of him. They presented the dead bodies of the kids to the whole community including the government officials, testifying that they saw the children killed by our Todd. He stood accused of these murders, and no one came to his defense. Throughout there were lies, fear, blackmail, and evil agreement. The community called for his arrest and imprisonment, so he fled for his life.

When I demanded, "What are you doing in this place?" Todd did not even think that I would believe the truth. He was, in a matter of speaking, tied upon a tree to die, the great man of God silenced, doomed to a life lost in the streets; his ministry destroyed, his reputation gone, his honor stripped.

## LADDER STEP 4: DESTRUCTION

We have now reached the height of the ladder. Pain and suffering are the result of destruction. The expression of evil at this stage requires the agreement of the people used. This is a true partnership in evil.

## VIOLENCE

Within the ladder, when anger is expressed, and developed along its path of hatred, rage and wrath, it most often manifests as violence.

Violence is the form of destruction causing the most damage of all.

> Gen.6:10 Now the earth was corrupt in the sight of God, and the earth was filled with **violence**.

> Proverbs 13:2 From the fruit of a man's mouth he enjoys good, But the desire of the treacherous is **violence**.

## DESTRUCTION: visible and invisible

### Visible Destruction (physical)

Destruction is seen in the world in wars and even acts of nature in general. It leaves a trail of property damage and death producing misery, suffering, hopelessness, despair etc.

After having a few arguments over the topic of the natural world being subject to evil, and the topic of God causing or not causing natural disasters, I have decided to avoid producing arguments and anger! So we will leave this topic out of our chapter!

> Isaiah 60:18 "**Violence** will not be heard again in your land, nor devastation or destruction within your borders; But you will call your walls salvation, and your gates praise.

## Invisible destruction

(mental, emotional and spiritual)

Most often evil activity is hidden in unseen manipulations that cause destruction, glorying in the injustice spewed upon the righteous. Invisible destruction can be experienced in lost hopes and dreams, in damaged faith in God, in ruined relationships, and in the disintegration of family bonds, all through manifesting evil.

This invisible destruction is propagated in the second heaven--the realm of spirits, where spiritual wickedness thrives. But it is exposed to our world through pride. This is the very being and nature of the evil one. His work is to kill, steal, and destroy, and he can't help but brag for he is proud of his work. His work generates fear, his favorite and most effective tool. His motivation is pride and hatred in its purest form. His time is short so he is in a cycle of increasing viciousness.

> Psalm 73:6 Therefore pride is their necklace; The garment of **violence** covers them.

I want to recount a true story of an extraordinary experience I had, in which God allowed me to see and experience the pride and arrogance that is always found in the Kingdom of evil.

While visiting a city that was surrounded by hills, our guide brought us to the top of the central hill, where we could look out upon the whole region. As I stood upon the ruins of the Temple of Hercules, I was swept into increasing darkness, experiencing the eerie movement of dots created from the newly lighted lamps spreading across the hills. Adding to the surreal atmosphere, the sounds of strange worship began to rise as the call to prayer echoed between the hills, in a naturally amplified sound that permeated the air in ever increasing intensity.

Suddenly, I found myself slowly shrinking downward into the size of an ant, and I saw satan looming before me as a swelling, puffing presence of evil, enjoying his worship. Swelling and deflating in harmony with the worship, he magnified the echoing sound throughout the hills. Satan was showing me his glories while practically begging me to worship him, thinking that he would be irresistible in his grandeur and magnificence.

Somewhere in the range of 2.5 million people were joining in agreement with the trumpeted calls of worship. Although not instituting the idolatry themselves, they were being used in the ritual, totally unaware of who it was they were bowing down to. "Shouldn't they have a chance to choose who they worship?" crossed my mind.

God then gave me this sentence to say to satan: “These hills (containing the people) will yet praise Jesus Christ and not you.” Looking at him from my minuscule height, I delivered the message, and then immediately grew back to my normal size. My companions and I got back into the car, and we drove down the mountain into the nighttime city.

> Proverbs 8:13 "The fear of the Lord is to hate evil; **Pride** and arrogance and the evil way and the perverted mouth, I hate.

## THE LADDER'S FUEL

Alcohol and drug abuse, leading to addictions and demonic possession, cause a large majority of the abuse and exploitation found in Step 4. Alcohol and drugs enable the whole ladder to activate on every level in concerted chaos, splattering the manifesting evil from all steps simultaneously. And so it might be argued that when people indulge even mildly in these substances they inadvertently aid the furtherance of evil by contributing to financial profit for the manufacturers of alcohol and illegal drugs. Can you occasionally drink alcohol and be in God's Kingdom? Yes, for the Bible tells us this :

> 1 Timothy 5:23 No longer drink water exclusively, but use a little **wine** for the sake of your stomach and your frequent ailments.

> Titus 2:3 Older women likewise are to be reverent in their behavior, not malicious gossips nor enslaved to much **wine**, teaching what is good,

1 Timothy 3:3 not addicted to **wine** or pugnacious, but gentle, peaceable, free from the love of money.

Ephesians 5:18 And do not get drunk with **wine**, for that is dissipation, but be filled with the Spirit,

**Fuel Stereotype Example:**

Suppose a simple man is an addict because of pain in his life caused by Step 1 manifesting evil.

When drunk or high he:

- He blames the boss who fired him for careless work (Step 2)
- He is full of anger at anyone trying to stop his behaviors. (Step 3)
- When drunk, he regularly beats his wife and children - violence, and He destroys their lives by using their funds for his addictions. (Step 4 Destruction)
- Having lost everything, he ends up at best alone, at worst dead from his addiction. (Step 5 Death)

Evil uses Deception, Fear, Blackmail, Pride, and Agreement, as its favored tools in keeping the people of the earth in bondage. Yet the power to set people free rests in Jesus Christ, for the "Truth Shall Set You Free." John 8:32

**God says:**

> Galatians 5:1 It was for freedom that Christ set us free; therefore keep standing firm and do not be subject again to a yoke of slavery.
>
> Galatians 5:13 For you were called to freedom, brethren; only do not turn your freedom into an opportunity for the flesh, but through love serve one another.
>
> Romans 8:21 that the creation itself also will be set free from its slavery to corruption into the freedom of the glory of the children of God.

# 5 DEATH

**5. Death**

4. Destruction

3. Anger

2. Blame

1. Evil manifesting

**Our Story Stops:**

The death of Todd's beloved street kids and the destruction of his ministry brought everything to a halt.

**LADDER STEP 5: DEATH**

Death is total separation from the God who loves you. Life is finished and all avenues to find "the way" out of the evil you have agreed to are closed. The chance for repentance and change are now over. When you die, your spirit goes to God, your soul goes to judgment, and your body goes to dust. Their fates are sealed.

Human souls will simply wait for their judgment with sorrow and wailing. Those who have been deceived into the rightness of their evil or find that they have spent their life in a false religion, worshiping demons, will be furious when they discover how they have been deceived away from the truth.

Tribes, countries and nations die by war, disease or conquest, or if they live, they continue to corrode through generations of hatred and rebellion, producing more destruction and death.

Rom 5:12 Therefore, just as through one man sin entered into the world, and death through sin, and so death spread to all men, because all sinned.

Death results in judgment.

Jn. 5:28,29 An hour is coming, when all who are in the tombs shall hear His voice, and shall come forth; those who did the good deeds to a resurrection of life, those who committed the evil deeds to a resurrection of judgment.

Death is a partner of hell and hades, reserved for the eternal lake of fire.

Revelation 20:13,14 And the sea gave up the dead which were in it, and **death** and **Hades** gave up the dead which were in them; and they were judged, every one of them according to their deeds. Then **death** and **Hades** were thrown into the lake of fire. This is the second death, the lake of fire.

In our story of Todd, death had won. Would there be a resurrection?

# 6. Escape

THE GREAT ESCAPE FROM THE LADDER OF EVIL

## Our Story's Outcome:

In my righteous anger I said to Todd, "NO WAY will they treat you like this. I absolutely refuse these circumstances. We are going to have honor and justice. You are deserving of nothing less than that!" I set the stage for five of us to converge upon the town of his injustice, within a period of about two weeks. I sent money, I arranged, and I pumped Todd with encouraging words. We arrived in the city on a Friday night, after the most trying of transportation issues.

For me, the trip started on the back of a motorcycle to the nearest town an hour away, where my escort and I could catch a ride. Here, we found there were only cars-for-hire at such an expensive rate it would take everyone's hotel money for the week to get to the city. I had to decide whether to go on, spending all that I had just to get there, or give up and go back. After some intense wrestling between my practical side and my conviction that this was what God wanted, I decided God could supply us, and on we went.

The trip for Todd and his escort was not as pleasant as mine. They took public buses from the other side of the country, and apparently were suffering from a virus that caused diarrhea! Many, many times they had to ask the bus drivers to stop so that they could run for the bushes, making the other bus passengers laugh, and have a little too much fun at their expense!

Upon arrival I found an internet café and wrote a passionate plea to my prayer people for money. Several people responded and I picked up money the following morning. America saved us once again!

Then we got to work. First, Todd and the team, after prayer, made an exploratory trip to the village. They found the original ex-witchdoctor who had become a Christian, and the eight-year-old boy who had been tied to the tree. And even though the street kids had abandoned the place to its evil, they found two former street kids and one family left in the village who welcomed Todd, and soon, me.

When I arrived, I found the ex-witchdoctor to be so ill with malaria that he could not move at all--even his mouth. We began to pray for him. He became somewhat better and able to talk. I asked him questions and then gently began to preach about the blood of Jesus, telling him of its great power over all evil.

We spent our last day there making plans, cleansing the land, and shooting video for future use. I asked the ex-witchdoctor if he wanted a new identity. He said yes. He chose a name before Todd took him to the hospital to be treated. When he was well, he moved to a new city to be trained as an ABU Street Pastor. Todd also took the boy who had been tied on a tree, and he is now happily registered in school for the first time. They live as a family, and they work on the streets protecting street kids and teaching them the ways of God.

The first report from our beloved ex-witchdoctor came in this week, just in time for me to share it with you:

> "Hello mom, how are doing? I hope our Lord Jesus Christ has kept you well.
>
> I am, a person who lived all his life as a witch doctor and i want everyone to know how Jesus Christ has changed me and where He is taking me. Before I got saved, I was a bad thing ever on this earth. I loved no-one but only had hatred in my heart. But now Jesus has given me love, feeling, hope, kindness and He taught me to know good and bad.....
>
> I love the street kids and I pray that God should let me be their guardian forever. I preach to them and pray for

them when they are sick. God loves children, so my kids often get healed if I pray for them .....I love that.

Yesterday I slept out with one of the kids who escaped from a great witch doctor who has been practicing witchcraft for many years and he want them dead now, just because they were his servants and escaped. These kids say that he killed their parents so he owned them and even promised to love them. But instead he trains them to kill and destroy. I found these kids on streets when they were about to die...when no one wants to touch them. And I prayed for them. Two of them have malaria .... very sick and they have serious wounds on their hands and legs because of the ropes he tied them with for two weeks in the shrine.

Mom I need money to leave the area with them, for them to be safe and get treatment.....please help. 250,000ugx. This evil man is hunting them down. It is an emergency. Please reply me soon... son"

## ESCAPING FROM THE EVIL LADDER

The path of escape was executed and purchased for us by Jesus Christ the Messiah.

> 1 John 3:8 the one who practices sin is of the devil; for the devil has sinned from the beginning. **The Son of God appeared for this purpose, to destroy the works of the devil.**

## THE GLORIUS PLAN

From the time of Adam:

Gen.25 Adam had relations with his wife again; and she gave birth to a son, and named him Seth, for, she said, "God has appointed me another offspring in place of Abel, for Cain killed him." 26 To Seth, to him also a son was born; and he called his name Enosh. Then men began to call upon the name of the LORD.

From Adam to Noah 10 generations
From Shem to Abraham 10 generations
From Abraham to David 14 generations
From David to the deportation to Babylon 14 generations. From
the deportation to Babylon to the Messiah, 14 generations

I gathered this information from Mat 1:17 to

show you how The Great Escape from the Evil Ladder was an ingenious plan of God, from eternity.

> Jer.1:5 "Before I formed you in the womb I knew you; before you were born I set you apart; I appointed you as a prophet to the nations."

How did the Son of God destroy the works of the devil? Being born as a human, He lived a sinless life of perfect obedience to the Father, right here in the midst of enemy territory. At the appointed time He gave up his life to his enemies for death, from which He rose again from the grave as a victor!

The path of escape is based upon this foundation: **"Without the shedding of blood there is no remission of sins"** (Hebrews 9:22). The escape path for each of us is currently waiting for our acceptance and belief in Jesus Christ the Son of God, who overcame the world through the shedding of His blood, pure and unstained by sin. Our belief and acceptance of His shed blood is shown by repentance for our sins, both personal and corporate.

## OVERCOMING

This is how Jesus overcame each ladder step:

1John5:5 Who is the one who overcomes the world, but he who believes that Jesus is the **Son of God**.

**Step 1. Evil Manifesting:** Jesus was betrayed unto death by Judas, one of His own disciples, on the very night that He instituted the New Covenant.

Mark 14:10 Then Judas Iscariot, who was one of the twelve, went off to the chief priests in order to betray Him to them.

**Step 2. Blame:** Jesus is **Blamed** for the truth! Jesus was accused by the Jews of blasphemy, because He called Himself the Son of God, which was the truth. This resulted in His death charge.

John 19:7 The Jews answered him, "We have a law, and by that law He ought to die because He made Himself out to be the **Son of God**."

Jesus said nothing to that charge. But later His title was recognized in public shame:

John 19:19 Pilate also wrote an inscription and put it on the cross. It was written, "JESUS THE NAZARENE, THE KING OF THE JEWS".

**Step 3. Anger:** The crowd became **Angry,** demanding his killing. Jesus silently suffered his people choosing a murderer for release instead of Him. Here we see mob justice in action.

> Matthew 27:22,23,26 Pilate said to them, "Then what shall I do with Jesus who is called Christ?" They all said, "Crucify Him!" And he said, "Why, what evil has He done?" But they kept shouting all the more, saying, "Crucify Him!" Then he released Barabbas for them; but after having Jesus scourged, he handed Him over to be crucified. And He spoke not a word.

**Step 4. Destruction:** Jesus allowed Evil to beat him, mock Him, crown Him with thorns, and then nail him on a tree to suffer, as the worst kind of sinner, hanging between two thieves. He endured the violence, blaming no one, and forgave all His abusers, saying, *"Father, Forgive them, for they know not what they do."* Lk 23:34

**Step 5. Death:** Jesus submitted to Evil, dying on a tree. He actually chose to give up His life--it was not taken from Him.

> Luke 23:46 "Into Your hands I commit My spirit".

This was the required blood sacrifice, and the only sufficient sacrifice, suffered by the Son of God for the sins of the world. *He took all the punishment we deserved, on our behalf*, so that he could conquer death for us.

Romans 8:3 For what the Law could not do, weak as it was through the flesh, God did: sending His own Son in the likeness of sinful flesh and as an offering for sin, He condemned sin in the flesh.

Two huge events were produced by his sacrificial death: 1. *the new covenant* in His blood, and 2. *the resurrection* into His new body. These two events affect all believers into eternity!

## 1. THE NEW COVENANT

With this blood sacrifice (as the Lamb that was slain), The *new covenant* in Jesus' blood was instituted for all peoples on earth. There would be no more temple and sacrifice ever needed again.

Old Testament prophecy of the new covenant:

Jeremiah 31:31,33,34 "Behold, days are coming," declares the Lord, "when I will make a **new covenant** with the house of Israel and with the house of Judah. [33] "But this is the covenant which I will make with the house of Israel after those days," declares the LORD, "I will put My law within them and on their heart I will write it; and I will be their God, and they shall be My people. [34] They will not teach again, each man his neighbor and each man his

> brother, saying, 'Know the LORD,' for they will all know Me, from the least of them to the greatest of them," declares the LORD, "for I will forgive their iniquity, and their sin I will remember no more."

The institution of the New Covenant:

> Luke 22:20 And in the same way He took the cup after they had eaten, saying, "This cup which is poured out for you is the covenant in my blood."

It is because of the new covenant that the rest of the world's peoples are invited into the Kingdom of God.

> Acts 2:21 And it shall be that everyone who calls on the name of the Lord will be saved.

## 2. THE RESURRECTION:

**Jesus' body did not see corruption after burial.**

In the three days that Jesus was "in the grave" He descended into hell and took the keys of Death and Hades away from the devil.

> Rev.1:17,18 And He placed His right hand on me, saying, "Do not be afraid; I am the first and the last, and the living One; and I was dead, and behold, I am alive forevermore, and I have the keys of death and of Hades.

> Ephesians4:9.10 (Now this expression, "He ascended," what does it mean except that He also had **descended** into the lower parts of the earth. He who **descended** is Himself also He who ascended far above all the heavens, so that He might fill all things.)

> 1Pet 3:19-20 ....in which also He (Jesus) went and made proclamation to the spirits now in prison, who once were disobedient, when the patience of God kept waiting in the days of Noah, during the construction of the ark, in which a few, that is, eight persons, were brought safely through the water.

In the three days that Jesus was "in the grave" Jesus ascended to heaven and presented His blood on the altar of sacrifice once eternally for all.

> Heb.9:11-14 But when Christ appeared as a high priest of the good things to come, He entered through the greater

> and more perfect tabernacle, not made with hands, that is to say, not of this creation; and not through the blood of goats and calves, but through His own blood, He entered the holy place once for all, having obtained eternal redemption. For if the blood of goats and bulls and the ashes of a heifer sprinkling those who have been defiled sanctify for the cleansing of the flesh, how much more will the blood of Christ, who through the eternal Spirit offered Himself without blemish to God, cleanse your conscience from dead works to serve the living God?

**Jesus arose in a new body on the third day.** He was seen on the earth for 40 days.

> Romans 1:4 who was declared the **Son of God** with power by the resurrection from the dead, according to the Spirit of holiness, Jesus Christ our Lord.

Jesus' resurrection brings these wonderful results for believers:

> John 11:25 Jesus said to her, "I am the **resurrection** and the life; he who believes in Me will live even if he dies."

> Rom.8:23 For the wages of sin is death, but the free gift of God is **eternal life** in

Christ Jesus our Lord.

John 5:24 "Truly, truly, I say to you, he who hears my word, and believes in Him who sent Me, has **eternal life** and does not come into judgment, but has passed out of death into life."

When Jesus was resurrected, many graves were opened and the dead came to life. This was a "first fruit" event, a foreshadowing of that glorious future event; the resurrection of our bodies when He returns. It was such an appropriate celebration for the conquering of death!!

Acts 1:3 To these He also presented Himself alive after His suffering, by many convincing proofs, appearing to them over a period of forty days and speaking of the things concerning the kingdom of God.

Matt 27:51-53 And behold, the veil of the temple was torn in two from top to bottom; and the earth shook and the rocks were split. 52 The tombs were opened, and many bodies of the saints who had fallen asleep were raised; 53 and coming out of the tombs after His resurrection they entered the holy city and appeared to many.

The Old Testament prophesy of these graves

being opened is found in this scripture:

> Ezekiel 37:13 Then you will know that I am the Lord, when I have opened your graves and caused you to come up out of your graves, My people.

The future fulfillment of graves being opened is found in these scriptures:

> Romans 8:19 For the anxious longing of the creation waits eagerly for the revealing of the sons of God.

> Luke 20:36 ....for they cannot even die anymore, because they are like angels, and are sons of God, being sons of the resurrection.

**Jesus left earth and ascended into the heavens:**

> Acts 1:9-11 He was lifted up while they were looking on, and a cloud received Him out of their sight. And as they were gazing intently into the sky while He was going, behold, two men in white clothing stood beside them. They also said, "Men of Galilee, why do you stand looking into the sky? This Jesus, who has been taken up from you into heaven, will come in just the same way as you have watched Him go into heaven."

## HOW THIS ENABLES US TO CONQUER EVIL

1. By believing in (trusting, submitting to) Jesus Christ and his accomplished work on our behalf, we follow Him in the path of escape that He made for us.

2. We then have access to the power the Holy Spirit freely gives to us, to conquer evil. We have power:

   - To refuse to blame....to forgive instead.
   - To spread the good news of Christ to those who have not heard.
   - To promote Jesus' ministry of peace.
   - To refuse to agree with evil, and to actively bring God's Kingdom to earth.

I love to write and preach Jesus more than anything else. It is my joy and passion. There is no greater story in this world than the one of Jesus Christ. It is called the "Good News", for it has the power to make each believer an OVERCOMER when mixed with faith. It is this which qualifies us to become the Bride of Christ. May all who read this book and apply its' knowledge to their sphere of influence, dwell in the secret place of the Most High.

# EPILOGUE

## ~~BLAME~~ - FORGIVENESS

The most difficult personal lesson for each of us I have saved for an epilogue. If we do not apply this lesson now, the reading of this book is a futile waste of time. To forgive is a choice, a choice that is hard. Only the love of God in our hearts can give us the power to forgive. This power is free but must be asked for.

There are two Greek words in the New Testament that are translated "forgiveness".

## 1. TO SEPARATE

G863 aphiemi verb; KJV - leave , forgive, suffer, let, forsake, let alone. 1

You could say; "I choose to separate myself from this offense committed against me instead of blame the cause."

Example:

Mk 11:25-26 And when you stand praying, forgive, (aphiemi) if you have ought against any: that your Father also which is in heaven may forgive you your trespasses. But if you do not forgive, neither will your Father which is in heaven forgive your trespasses.

## 2. RELEASE

The second Greek word is G859 aphesis noun KJV- remission, forgiveness, deliverance, liberty; 1) release from bondage or imprisonment; forgiveness or pardon, of sins (letting them go as if they had never been committed), remission of the penalty. 2

Example:

> Ac 26:18 - To open their eyes, and to turn them from darkness to light, and from the power of Satan unto God, that they may receive forgiveness of sins, and inheritance among them which are sanctified by faith that is in Me.

Next we will study the three types of sin, translated in the Old Testament as:

1.Transgressions (soulish/self, separation, rebellion)

2. Iniquities (spiritual separation)

3. Sins (fleshly rebellion)

> Exodus 34:7 God keeps mercy for thousands, forgiving iniquity (spiritual separation) and transgression (soulish/self separation, rebellion) and sins (fleshly rebellion), and will by no means clear the guilty. We are exploring

these sins to enlighten our understanding of how they corrupt our inner being. After taking a look at sin within our own self, maybe we will find it easier to let go of the things we've gathered up against others. This sets us free to explore LOVE, through the avenue of forgiveness.

## HEART of the BORN AGAIN

Genesis 1:26a -Then God said, "Let Us (Father, Son, Holy Spirit) make man in Our image, according to Our likeness; let them have dominion"

John 3:15-16 - whoever believes in Him should not perish but have eternal **life.** For God so loved the world that He gave His only begotten Son, that whoever believes in Him should not perish but have everlasting **life**.

1 Thessalonians 5:23 - Now may the God of peace Himself sanctify you completely; and may your whole spirit, soul, and body be preserved blameless at the coming of our Lord Jesus Christ.

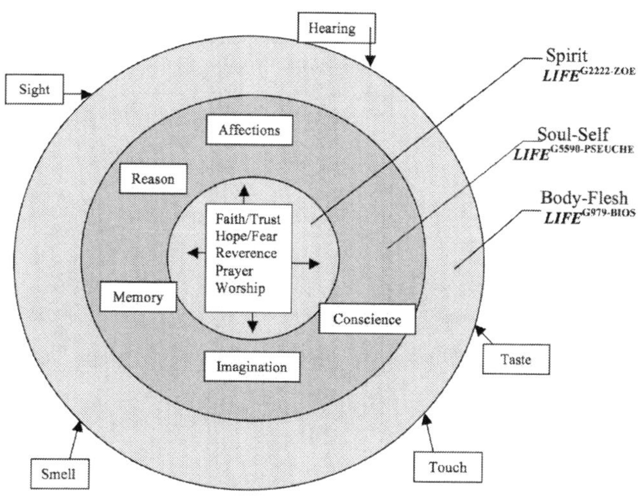


- Inputs to the Body-Flesh are from the gates (senses): Taste, Touch, Smell, Sight, and Hearing.

- Inputs to the Soul-Self are from: Imagination, Conscience, Memory, Reason, and Affections.

- Inputs from the Spirit are: Faith/Trust, Hope, Reverence, Prayer, and Worship.

- The input from the Spirit purifies our imagination, cleanses our conscience, restores memories of our true origins, aligns our reasoning, and directs our affections always to God first. It allows us not to be victims of the senses that bombard our flesh, but rather to become a discerning spirit.

Exodus 34:7 - God keeps mercy for thousands, forgiving iniquity (spiritual separation) and transgression (soulish/self separation, rebellion) and sin (fleshly rebellion), and will by no means clear the guilty.

## HEART of the UNSAVED

Genesis 3:6 - So when the woman saw that the tree *was* good for food (G979), that it was pleasant to the eyes (G5590), and a tree desirable to make *one* wise, she took of its fruit and ate.

1 John 2:15-17 - "Do not love the world or the things in the world. If anyone loves the world, the love of the Father is not in him. For all that *is* in the world; the lust of the flesh (G979), the lust of the eyes (G5590), and the pride of life; is not of the Father but is of the world. And the world is passing away, and the lust of it; but he who does the will of God abides forever."

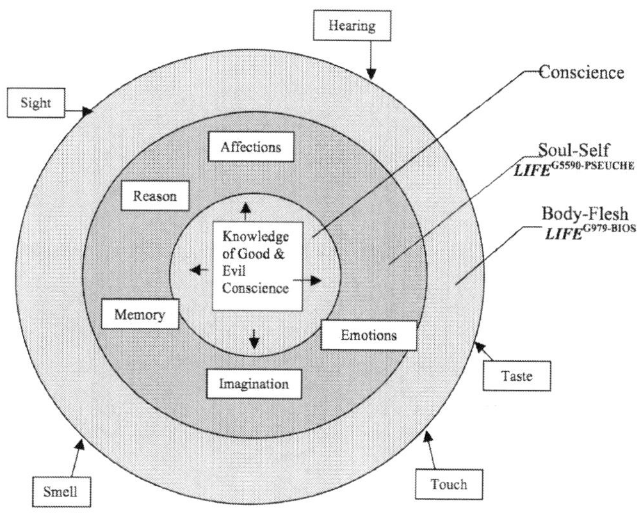


- Inputs to the Body-Flesh are from the **gates** (senses): Taste, Touch, Smell, Sight, and Hearing.

- Inputs to the Soul-Self are from: Imagination, Conscience, Memory, Reason, and Affections.

- The SOUL is the MIND, WILL & EMOTIONS. The WILL being the 'door' between the Conscience and the SOUL.

- The input from the Knowledge of the Tree of Good & Evil puts iniquity in our imagination, makes our conscience unclean, causes us to forget memories of our true origins, misaligns our reasoning, and directs our affections to the world, the flesh and the devil. It allows us to be victims of the senses that bombard our flesh. 3

Exodus 34:7– God keeps mercy for thousands, forgiving iniquity (spiritual separation) and transgression (soulish/self separation, rebellion) and sin (fleshly rebellion), and will by no means clear the guilty.[2]

---

1.Strong's Exhaustive Concordance of the Bible, (Royal Publishers, Inc., 1979)
2.Ibid
3. John Munns - Therapon

# THE LACE

# THE LACE

Touch, oh God, our inner hearts with your most blessed grace.
Making changes deep inside creates new threads of lace.
A piece of lace, a gift for You, that You might celebrate,
The beauty of a family of LOVE, devoid of hate.

Come down, oh LOVE, and capture us, as those caught unaware,
While even in this dance of twisting threads of pain we bear.
Retie those threads- a tapestry of beauty meant to be;
The lace, of past and present too, a work of beauty we.

Eternal consequences lie within a heart reborn.
Reborn, for nothing of our hearts is worthy to adorn
Your paths of thread, entwining those whose testimonies given,
Have helped so many come to You, with new joy in their living.

How do You bear corruption here, among Your chosen ones;
While playing games of tainted sin, with evil quickly done?
Yet Eden calls! The lovely lace of fun and joy has won!
Until the thread is called to give its life, to save a son.

Broken, twisted, frayed, and damaged—can it live again?
Beside that awful broken thread—a new thread is laid in!
Repentance and Forgiveness make the thread of Love move on.
Not stopping for its rest until, Your smile of joy is won!

Jane Snyder
March 2014

# ABOUT THE AUTHOR

Jane Snyder is a piano teacher and church musician who carries a heart for the Nations. She did prayer events using all of the arts for over fifty countries, but now works in those countries bringing help to street kids. Her ministry to the abandoned called Active Blessing, is an arm of Melchizedek's Treasure Ltd. Her passion is the transformation of abandoned children. www.ActiveBlessing.com

Made in the USA
Middletown, DE
21 July 2016